Thriving Success

in Life & Business Series

10 Things You MUST Have

Book One

Passion

By Steve Kidd
Foreword by Dr. Donald M. Joy

Thriving *Success Series* – Passion

by Steve Kidd

© 2015 Steve Kidd (www.wehelpyouthrive.com). All content is copyrighted and all rights are reserved. No reproduction of any content is permitted without written consent.

This information is given to help you grow. It is presented to help you examine your life and know some elements that are needed for success. No guarantee of success written or implied comes with this information. It is however created with a genuine desire to see you succeed in life and in business!

Thriving *Success Series* – Passion

Thriving *Success Series* – Passion

Contents

Foreword 6

Introduction..11

A topic or niche you are passionate about.................19

Zombie..26

Passion awakens the true you...................................28

Define your passion 33

Start out right 43

Conclusion 46

Thriving *Success Series* – Passion

Thriving *Success Series* – Passion

Foreword

Steve Kidd is a pro. He lives in the Pacific Northwest. I live in the Kentucky Bluegrass. He speaks with authority about choosing men- tors across the life span. I am honored to have mentored Steve throughout most of his life, starting when he stayed with Robbie and me in 3rd grade. Steve has navigated his share of challenges. Steve knows how to scramble, rearrange, upgrade, and maintain his pastoral ministry and his businesses along with his personal challenges without dropping parishioners, customers, clients, and family members.

I knew Steve's entire family. His parents earned graduate credit in a Monday graduate

Thriving *Success Series* – Passion

credit lunch-hour seminar I facilitated as we developed parent guides for discussing meaning with children for each of C. S. Lewis' six Chronicles of Narnia.

When Steve was in seventh grade, he signed on for a week of back-country backpacking in the lower Appalachia Mountains in eastern Kentucky on the Sheltowee Trace. During that week he settled into a trail family hosted by three of my graduate students expecting to become youth ministers.

Steve and four other middle school guys stretched to draw energy and imagination from those three men 24/7 for ten days. For the last three days, they set up their tarp and spread their ground cloths in rain. They broke camp and cooked breakfast in the rain. They hiked all day in the rain.

Thriving *Success Series* – Passion

Early August backpacking is manageable in the rain, if you have a parka that waterproofs you and your backpack. But wet clothes and socks accumulate. And wet stuff is heavy. We operated a "chuck-wagon" which intercepted us each evening at a highway. The driver set up tarps to cover the cook-wagon and extra lean- to tarps to cover campers as they ate. I suggested that campers off-load their wet clothing in a plastic trash bag, label it, load it on the chuck-wagon, then pick it up at the end of the trail before boarding the bus back to campus.

My memory image of Steve at thirteen is of a happy camper, ambling up the hill to my house to find me. His parents were waiting a block away, anxious waiting take him back to Indiana where they were now

Thriving *Success Series* – Passion

living. The bright sunny Kentucky day was pale compared to Steve's face radiant, satisfied, confident, innocent.

I was working in the garage and Steve saw it open. Robbie and I were sorting and folding freshly laundered clothing quickly retrieved from a half dozen unclaimed garbage bags heavy with wet clothing.

"Hello, Dr. Joy," he said. "I forgot to pick up my wet clothes and my mother is upset with me." Robbie, who had been mumbling about "careless children," morphed into Steve's helper as he sorted through freshly laundered clothing. He identified all of his clothes, and returned home, forever our friend.

Fast forward to Steve's Pacific coast ministry career and his entrepreneurial businesses.

Thriving *Success Series* – Passion

Steve e-mailed me an offer to set up a website for me. "I have several clients. I manage their sites for them, and I would like to set up a site for you and manage it for you as my gift to you." I wanted it mostly to make it an identity site with free downloads of my out of print books and links to my publishers who market my books. Steve wanted my books and information preserved and has happily hosted and maintained my website for 10 years.

Today, at 87, I am thankful for Steve and for his ministry, his resilience, and his expertise. He has 10 THINGS worth brooding over. I commend each of the books in this series to you.

Donald M. Joy, Professor of Human Development and Family Studies, Asbury Theological Seminary, Wilmore, Kentucky

Thriving *Success Series* – Passion

Introduction

Hi! My name is Steve Kidd, a third generation minister and business coach. I have been a business owner most all of my life. Throughout my life, I have been blessed to be mentored by some amazing people. So much of who I am today is thanks to the valuable life lessons other people have invested in me. In this book I hope to pass on even a little of the unique brilliance they have taught me.

As honored as I am by the impact the men and women who have poured into me have brought, this doesn't mean it has always been easy. I grew up very poor. You don't normally think about your pastor having any financial

Thriving *Success Series* – Passion

struggles, but the truth is many men and women who give themselves in ministry do so for very little financial gain.

I have memories of the times when there was quite literally no food in the house. My mom was amazing at always putting food on the table, but often it was literally making something out of next to nothing.

Now the thing about it is I really didn't know this growing up. It was only a few years ago when retelling the story that the truth of our circumstance came to light.

For me our meager existence only meant opportunity. If you wanted something you had to make it or earn the money to get it. This is where my journey as an entrepreneur began.

Thriving *Success Series* – Passion

I began my selling door-to-door at the age of 5. I learned early what it took to have money for things. I also fell in love with the advantages of self-employment. That was how and where I started and I have been selling in one form or another ever since.

Flash forward a little to 1988. I was young parent with little children I now needed to provide for. I wish I could tell you that by then I was independently wealthy, but in truth I was a young parent learning how to meet the needs of the little people whose lives were in my care.

So what did I do?

You guessed it I was self-employed. It was what knew. I was selling the newly developed laptop computer to professionals like insurance

Thriving *Success Series* – Passion

salesmen who were discovering the benefits technology can bring to their business.

I love technology. I love what it can do for us. But I also know that technology, like so many other things, tends to not be communicated well. Sometimes I think people in technology think there is an award for confusing people. From the early days I loved explaining business tools in an approachable and understandable manner for the average person.

I am blessed to work with my amazing wife Kathy, who is a true business strategist. She has a talent for researching and developing action plans that help people break through the things that have them stuck to a whole new level in life and in business.

It is so fun to use my passion to help you

Thriving *Success Series* – Passion

reframe things that seem like obstacles into possibilities. My mentors helped me to see that I have always had an ability to reach people where they are. To bring complicated things "down to earth" in an easy to understand and execute manner.

Then on day in late October of 2015 while helping a client write their Best Selling Book, I looked at the notes I had been taking and said, "You have an amazing story. Would you like to hear it?"

That moment God showed up, destiny revealed itself, my talent sprang forth. Whatever way you want to say it, that changed the course of my life and our business. I don't know why God chooses to give us the gifts He does. I am grateful for mine.

Through the course of an hour or so in an

Thriving *Success Series* – Passion

interview I help people bring out their story And at the end of that time I can literally read their story back to them. Through a seemingly casual conversation the book that needs to come out does!

I love helping people share their unique brilliance with the world. To bring out of them that specialness that the world so badly needs. To emphasis that one thing we all need to share with the world – OUR PASSION

I hope some of this book and the books in this series can do some of that for you as well.

Kathy and I are the ultimate one, two punch for your success in life and business. Kathy has had her struggles too. And I am sure in her books she will tell you about them. She has gone from someone diagnosed with agorapobia

Thriving *Success Series* – Passion

and unable to leave her house, to a person who now speaks regularly on the internet and YES even live on stage.

I am blessed that we met while helping a mutual client and have been able to bring our passions for business into a combined powerhouse team to serve you. We hope her story and mine will help you in your journey as you live an inspired life's and THRIVE!

We would love for you to join us any time on my radio show Thriving Entrepreneur or in our group BestSellersGuild.com.

This is book one. It is about *PASSION.* You will find that your passion is what drives you and is the cornerstone for anything else you do. As in each of the books there are a few simple keys that are a few of the traits I have found in

Thriving *Success Series* – Passion

common among highly successful people. Som of these things I have found you MUST have i order to not just survive, but to thrive an grow.

My desire in writing this is to provide you some simple actions and attitudes you can use so that you do not just have to "make it," or "have a go at it" but to truly have a company and a life full of success and happiness.

As you read each of the books in this series, don't let any of the 10 things cause you to fall into either the trap of striving for perfectionism, or the trap of self-judgment and criticism. These items are here to help you live your best life.

Kathy and I invite you to take this journey with us!

Thriving *Success Series* – Passion

A topic or niche you are passionate about

Your work and life need to be filled with things you love and are truly passionate about. It is always so much easier to push yourself if you are doing something you are always talking about. You have to do something you love.

I have heard so many people say they are motivated by money. Unless you are a billionaire money manager, that probably isn't true. If you were truly motivated by money then you would be doing everything in your power to have more money.

Thriving *Success Series* – Passion

Money versus your unique passion. - A person who has made a lot of money like Warren Buffet could be thought to say he was money motivated. However in a quote from his son Peter we learn that Warren Buffet encouraged following your passion.

"[My Dad] always said, 'Do what you love,'" says Peter. "That was critical. Really, my Dad and I do the same thing … He told me:'Don't settle for anything other than your passion – if you're lucky enough to find it." But finding it, Peter says, is the hardest part. [1]

When we say we are motivated by money what

[1] From "Warren Buffett's Son: 5 Lessons from Dad - http://www.cbsnews.com/8301-505123_162-51436499/warren-buffetts-son-5-lessons-from-dad/?tag=mwuser

Thriving *Success Series* – Passion

we mean is we are motivated by the personal outcomes we dream of having IF we had the money.

All of us have a life we want to live; a dream that we want to fulfill. In most cases this dream does involve money to be able to make our dream a reality. But it is the desire for those things in life that motivate us, not the money. The Disney version of Scrooge McDuck swimming in his money depicts a person who is money motivated. He doesn't want to spend it or do anything with it; he just wants money.

So ask yourself questions. Take the time to get serious with yourself. What is it that you are truly passionate about? For a moment forget about how much it costs and take the time to define what truly motivates you.

Thriving *Success Series* – Passion

It is imperative in life and in your business that long before you come up with a plan or even an idea that you know who you are. You need to know what makes you tick. What gets you up in the morning? Once you have taken the time to know yourself and know what you truly, want believe, desire and will do then you are truly ready to do great things in life or in business because you are doing them as the best thing you can be—YOU!

Often we stop dreaming realistically because the fantasy dreams of winning the lottery, striking it rich are so much easier than the work that is involved in success. Why? Because we can hide in an unreal fantasy. Our fantasy land is something that we get with no effort. It is a place where everything is perfect and all our desires are given to us. The truth is you CAN have any life you want! That's right:

Thriving *Success Series* – Passion

any- thing your mind can conceive, you can acquire.

There are two questions that determine whether you will succeed:

1. Are you willing to do what must be done in order to achieve your desire?
2. Would having this desire make you the best version of yourself?

Many of us never reach for our dreams because we have never been motivated enough to do what is necessary to reach our goal.

You want to win a huge sweepstakes?
- Is it humanly possible to enter enough times to make this dream a reality?
- Do you know the number of times you would have to enter to be assured you will win?

Thriving *Success Series* – Passion

- Can you realistically enter that many times?
- How many times is "enter as often as you like" limited to?
- How do they select the winners?
- And, of course, how many total entries will they receive?

If you haven't even done the research then is a safe bet to say that you are hiding in a fantasy and not really wanting something that you are willing to do what it takes to achieve.

Then of course there is the question of what you will be like if you do put all of your effort into this goal.

- Will it make you a better person?
- More importantly, will you be living a life that is the best version of yourself?

Thriving *Success Series* – Passion

- Will you be utilizing fully all your potential?
- Will all of your time and talent be completely integrated and in used in your daily life if you reach this goal?

These are important questions to ask when defining our true motivation because in the end we can lie to everyone else and we can even get good enough at it that we begin to fool ourselves. The problem is that inside we will not be fulfilled. We will not be using all of who we are and the parts that aren't being used will feel left out. This leads to an internal growing sense of unhappiness because the truth is that life is not about reaching an end goal, it is about living.

Thriving *Success Series* – Passion

Zombie

The saddest thing to see in life is a true

zombie. A zombie is a being who is dead but still up walking around. You have probably met (or even been) a zombie. They have reached a place in life where they have "arrived," "made it," or in some way completed all they have set out to do in life. These are the most miserable, lifeless people on the planet. They don't like themselves, they don't like their own lives and normally they don't tend to like anyone else either.

This wonderful victory lane called "retirement" in the Game of Life™ becomes a place of defeat and often death because there is nothing more

Thriving *Success Series* – Passion

to do, no more dreams to dream, no more mountains to climb, nothing more to accomplish than to watch the clock tick by until you draw your last breath.

No one wants this horrible zombie existence and yet all too often we find ourselves living our life like reaching "success" and sitting there basking in it is the goal for which we are headed.

Thriving *Success Series* – Passion

Passion awakens the true you.

What we really should be wanting to achieve is a true perspective of who we are so that we can then know ourselves. From this self-awareness comes the beginning spark of passion because we can identify who we are and what we truly are passionate about.

- What are the things you can never get enough of?
- What are the things that leave you feeling happy and wanting to do more?
- What activity, ideas and actions challenge you to use every bit of your energy to see it accomplished?

You shouldn't settle for anything less than a personal definition of who you are and what

Thriving *Success Series* – Passion

you are passionate about. Life and business should always be first and foremost based in finding and reaching something that excites you and takes every fiber of your being to accomplish.

Our passion shows up through our actions. It shows up because it is that thing that we are always doing, thinking about, and talking about. Life experience or can make us even become shy about expressing (or continuing to express) your real passion. The opposite can also be true. We may catch ourselves rambling on even after we notice others aren't really interested. With true passion it is not uncommon to find that people keep telling us we talk about it too much, still it keeps coming out.

You lie in bed thinking about it. You plan how to

Thriving *Success Series* – Passion

make it a reality. Even when you have tried to stop thinking about it, it is always just there. It is almost as though it creeps into your mind and thoughts all by itself.

Ever felt that way? Well, I say GO FOR IT!

This is the real, complete you. This is the thing that engages all of who you are. It isn't just you doing something you are good at: it is you completely dedicated to being YOU!

As I sit here typing this, I am actually watching my beautiful wife put this very thing into action. It has been a long week. It is later at night than we should be up and she is tired physically, but right now she is fully engaged in her passion. She is engaged in what she is doing with all of who she is. She is completely present right here in this moment focused on

Thriving *Success Series* – Passion

the project she is working on. She is aglow with the joy of it and frankly, if she stayed up all night I wouldn't be shocked at all.

Because when all of who we are is engaged in what we are doing, there is nothing that can stop us. There is no energy drink or supplement that can touch the energy we get when we are fully engaged in being fulfilled in what we are passionate about. Most importantly there is nothing we can't achieve and no greater happiness than being on the road that allows us to live this kind of life.

The funny part of it is while she sits across the desk from me at her desk fully engaged, I too am also living the best version of me that I can right here, right now! Fully and completely living a life filled with passion! I am living my best life, even as a write to you about living

Thriving *Success Series* – Passion

yours.

Thriving *Success Series* – Passion

Define your passion

So maybe you are wondering how this applies to your business. The first thing you need to do is to de- fine your passion. Then, you have to accept that until you find a way to be that person you will never be totally happy. After you accept these basic principles in life then you have to choose what you are going to do. Passion must be your basis.

The biggest mistake I see people make is choosing a business because it is trendy, thus thinking they will make a lot of money with it. There are a couple of problems with this approach.

First off, trends change. What is popular today probably won't be this time next year. You may

Thriving *Success Series* – Passion

make some money for a while on a hot topic but after a while you will find that interest has waned and your audience has moved on.

Trends are going to change. The way the real you is expressed in life is likely to change over time as well. You probably don't have a typewriter any more. Probably you have a computer. The ways you exist, the house you live in, the age you are, and the experiences you have had will change, but the heart and soul of who you are won't.

I have been blessed to know some people who have made money—lots of money—some through traditional business and some online. The ways they have made their money probably span most every approach that exists. Most of them will gladly tell you how they did it and even help you be successful too.

Thriving *Success Series* – Passion

Here is the sad part:

I know hundreds of people who know IN DETAIL exactly what these people did. They have had it shown to them step by step. Sadly, even with knowing how they could do it, and why it works, people don't do it.

Why?

Because in the end it was not something they were passionate about. Because they lacked the passion for it, they either never found the time to do it or quit before they ever saw any significant success from it.

You will find in life that success always follows passion.

Thriving *Success Series* – Passion

Second, and more important, if you aren't inspired by the topic you will find that not only has your audience left, but so have you. If you love what you do, then in the tough times your love for it can help you find a reason to do the things you don't want to do.

On the other hand without passion it is just a job. Without having your true self in it then it is just an idea you came up with, or something you thought would be successful. When the hard times come I can tell you from experience when you are working on something like that then anything and everything will continue to be more interesting.

Have you ever worked a job you didn't like? If you have then you know what I mean. Any reason to not go to work is a good reason.

The same is true with your business. If you are

Thriving *Success Series* – Passion

passionate about what you are doing, on the bad days your passion will help you and on the good days will make you feel overwhelmingly fulfilled.

I worked with a company that spent over 7 million (yes MILLION!) dollars on a project because "it was a good idea and something the market needed."

You know what they did with it once it was finished?

They stopped the whole thing!

Even though the project was completed and working, the company abandoned it. All the people on the project were either let go or moved to other divisions. All of these people in that department walked away.

Thriving *Success Series* – Passion

Even after the company had spent over 7 million dollars. In spite of the fact that they had several years of planning and development invested in this one project; nothing was ever done with it.

Was it because the code wasn't any good?

No.

Was it because the market had changed and the idea was no longer applicable?

No.

It was for one simple reason: It was something practical, but not born out of passion. The one person in the company who had the passion for the project had been promoted. Even with all of that investment, without the passion propelling

Thriving *Success Series* – Passion

it, it fell by the wayside.

So, first off when choosing a business, pick something that you can't stop thinking about. Pick something you dream about. Then find out how you can make that dream into a business.

We all have responsibilities in life. If you are like many of us, you may be starting your business while working another (or even a couple of other) jobs. We all have bills to pay and people we love that we want spend time with. I am not a proponent of being a workaholic. To overwork and neglect your health and family is a recipe for a much worse life.

We need to have balance. I am not suggesting that having passion is an excuse to be an out-of-control, selfish person who sacrifices everything and everyone around them in order

Thriving *Success Series* – Passion

to reach their goal. Instead, we need to use the knowledge of what we are passionate about to make us even better people.

Our passion should propel us toward an even greater life. Our passion should be channeled into something that has the potential to replace the work we have to do with work that we love to do.

We all have real lives. And often all of us find ourselves not living our best life. We neglect our passion. We all have times when we make excuses for why we don't live a life that is built and based upon knowing who we are. It is easier to live a life that does not have an outlet for our passion. It is a common human condition for us to become so bogged down in the "have-to's" of living that we forget to live a life of passion.

Thriving *Success Series* – Passion

If we do know what our passion is and create a life that allows us to truly live as the best most passionate version of ourselves, it is easy to just let life and our surroundings dictate who and what we are. Soon we find ourselves living a life where days, months, even years go by without a thought for what it means to live our best life.

We need to think how we could exercise our passion daily. It is in the breakthrough of realizing that we must be as much of our authentic self as we can be every day that we find real joy in life and the ability to

Thriving *Success Series* – Passion

persevere.

We want to build a business that is designed as an outlet for our true self. We need to live life where our passionate whole being is the core of all we do. A business with what we are passionate about is a business that is built from the beginning to succeed.

Thriving *Success Series* – Passion

Start out right

Remember what starts out right ends up right; but what starts out wrong may never get right. Start off by identifying your passion. Then take the time to find a way to have your authentic self as the central hub on which everything you do is based.

Maybe you love to make people's lives better. There are millions of very useful products from vacuum cleaners to supplements that you could sell; not as the one and only solution that will change the world, but rather as a great product that will make your life better. Here is a company you want to buy from because the heart and soul of our company is not our product, it is our desire to improve your life.

Thriving *Success Series* – Passion

Maybe you love to preach or teach or write. Again there are a millions products you can sell or books you can write and make for sale, but the core of your business is that you love to use your words to impact people's lives. You desire to help them acquire knowledge or give them solutions to problems, or to gain a new skill set. Whatever the real passionate, driving force behind the why you love to do this should be the basis on which you build your whole company.

Then you are simply using your business cash flow as a means to pay you for the right, for the joy of getting to live every day as YOU! Not just some of you but all of the true authentic you—the unique person you were created to be.

Businesses come and go. Sometimes we start

Thriving *Success Series* – Passion

down one business path and find ourselves ending up in a different place. We don't need to fight the trends and changes in the world. We just simply need to have at the core our passion. We need to base our decisions on being true to ourselves. Take the time to know who you are and then invest in you.

If we use our true self as the criteria for our life, as well as our business decisions, then we will not only have a business that is succeeding, but, more important, we will truly be alive.

Don't skip step one! Find your passion. Know who you are and what you are passionate about. Then always make sure that everything you do first off in your life and then with your business is based on being true to yourself by always being true to your passion.

Thriving *Success Series* – Passion

Conclusion

I am so excited to release book one to you. I know that by living your passion everything you do in life will be better.

Though this series started as nothing more than a simple list, it has grown into an entire journey I can take with you.

As others have shared their wisdom and brilliance with me, it is my delight to pass it on to you. I hope you will stick with us through the whole series. You can read the books and take it from there or you can join our group BestSellersGuild.com as we take it even deeper.

This book is not intended to create perfect

Thriving *Success Series* – Passion

people. I didn't write it to claim I am an expert who never has struggles or makes mistakes. Each book in this series is both a part of who I am and who I strive to be daily.

This life is about continuing to grow. Just as this book series has grown from a simple list, as you read and reread it; as you join our group and go deeper; as you make thriving a part of your life; that you will find new things that you did not see each time.

The key is to commit to living a life where your passion is discovered, enhanced and continually growing.

Do not read this book and feel condemned. Do not judge yourself by the areas you are currently working on. Do not fall into the trap of trying to be perfect. Just live your life the

Thriving *Success Series* – Passion

best you know how, and use this book to help you discover new ways to learn and grow.

Here's to your continued life of success!
Be blessed!

In His Name

Steve Kidd

Thriving *Success Series* – Passion

Thriving *Success Series* – Passion

www.ingramcontent.com/pod-product-compliance
Lightning Source LLC
Chambersburg PA
CBHW050025230526
45470CB00003B/1129